KU-435-806

CONTENTS

EVERYDAY JAPANESE CHARACTERS

by
MICHAEL PYE

DUCKWORTH

First published in the United Kingdom in 1980 by
Gerald Duckworth & Company Limited
The Old Piano Factory
43 Gloucester Crescent, London NW1

First published in Japan in 1977 by
The Hokuseido Press

ISBN 0 7156 1514 9 (cased)
ISBN 0 7156 1515 7 (paper)

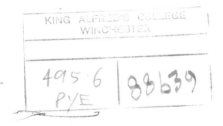

Printed and bound in Great Britain by
REDWOOD BURN LIMITED
Trowbridge & Esher

Most people who visit Japan for a short time pick up some useful words and phrases, and many who stay longer learn to speak the language quite fluently. Yet when it comes to the written language there is a lot of pessimistic head-shaking. This need not be so. Learning to read fluently is a laborious business, but the alternative is not complete illiteracy.

This little book makes few demands and gives quite practical information about some of the written characters met in daily life about Tokyo and other Japanese cities. Anyone wishing to study them more seriously and systematically should turn to my book *The Study of Kanji* (Hokuseido Press 1971), but even the following pages will lead to some reduction in daily inconvenience. Almost all the characters included can soon be picked out on signs and posters about town.

Characters from China

The characters used in writing Japanese originally came from China, but we are dealing with them only in so far as they form part of the Japanese language. In Japanese they are called KANJI ('CHINESE LETTERS') and that is how we refer to them from now on.

A KANJI may be read in one or more different ways. Some readings are native Japanese words and others are Japanese pronunciations of the Chinese words which the characters originally represented. Fluent readers have to distinguish these and to know when each of the various possibilities is intended. However the readings given in this book are just those appropriate to the context, or the ordinary conversational word associated with the KANJI.

Visual information

There may be some people with a predominantly visual memory who would prefer not to bother with pronunciations anyway. After all, it is possible to recognise and understand a KANJI without being able to 'read' it at all in the ordinary sense of the word. Perhaps you have seen Japanese abroad in Hongkong or Singapore, for example, who quickly work out the meaning of signs all over the place without having the slightest idea of how to pronounce them in Chinese. Similarly a Chinese person in Japan knows perfectly well that

means RAIN, even though he may not know what the Japanese *say* for RAIN. For most people however the spoken word is a useful reminder rather than a hindrance.

Pronunciation

Pronunciation cannot easily be explained in a book and nothing will be attempted here beyond four rules: consonants as in English, vowels as in Italian, long vowels must be long, double consonants must be double. If possible ask a Japanese friend to pronounce a few typical words for you. Conversational Japanese is taught in other books.

Romanisation

The rule 'consonants as in English' assumes the Hepburn system of romanising Japanese, which is used in this book. This system is authorised by the Ministry of Education for transliterating place names (e.g. on railway stations) and for other purposes relating to foreigners. There are also two other systems of romanisation, one of which is taught in all primary schools, but neither of which has any real practical application. This leads to a certain amount of confusion, but don't let it get you down.

Phonetic script

The HIRAGANA and KATAKANA 'alphabets' are two auxiliary phonetic systems of 46 symbols each, and either system represents perfectly all the sounds of the Japanese language. HIRAGANA and KATAKANA are known collectively as KANA.

In modern Japanese the HIRAGANA are combined with KANJI for ordinary writing and the KATAKANA are used mainly for words of foreign origin including many scientific and commercial words. You will notice that the HIRAGANA are smooth and flowing, in fact suitable for cursive writing, and that the KATAKANA are simpler and sharper in line.

A short-term visitor to Japan may find it more

interesting to get to know a few KANJI than to learn all the syllabic signs. In this case the frequently met advice that it is 'necessary' to learn the latter first may be disregarded. Anyone staying in the country a little longer however should make the effort to master them, as they will prove useful in a hundred and one ways.

Tables and notes for the HIRAGANA and KA-TAKANA are given in Chapter XXVIII, right at the end of this book, for easy reference. A few phonetic characters appear here and there in other chapters too, but equivalents in Roman letters are given every time as well.

Kanji

You may like to know that the basic number of KANJI for general use taught to all Japanese school-children is 1850. In the first six years of schooling they are supposed to learn 881 of these, namely the 'education kanji'. Widely used dictionaries containing literary, historical and other terms contain several thousand different ones, and the total number of KANJI which have been used at some time or other is something in the region of 40,000.

This pocket-book has been written in the modest belief that it is entertaining and handy to recognise even a few of these characters. The commoner ones appear again and again and again, and it only needs a few minutes each day and a little enthusiasm to begin to pick them out.

Good luck!

Further on you will find various groups of useful kanji to be found in everyday contexts. But first it may be as well to get some idea of how kanji were composed and built up into their present forms.

Many of the most fundamental ones began as pictures, and even now, if we let our imagination loose, we can often see the connection between shape and meaning. Take for example the kanji for RAIN (AME) mentioned in the Introduction:

雨

If you look at it for a moment you can almost see the water dripping out of the sky. It probably originated something like this (the last form being the modern one):

RAIN ... AME

Here are a few others which are thought to have developed somewhat as indicated:

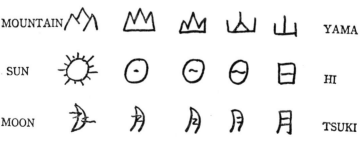

MOUNTAIN ... YAMA

SUN ... HI

MOON ... TSUKI

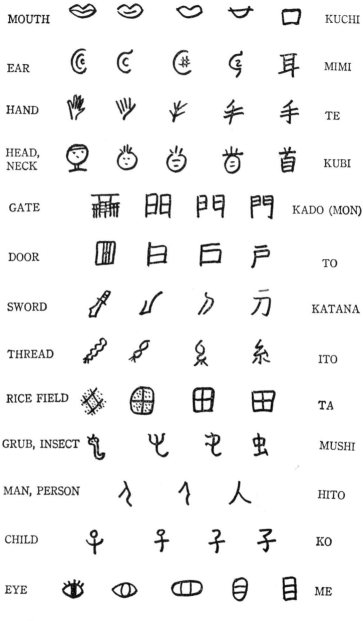

MOUTH						KUCHI
EAR						MIMI
HAND						TE
HEAD, NECK						KUBI
GATE						KADO (MON)
DOOR						TO
SWORD						KATANA
THREAD						ITO
RICE FIELD						TA
GRUB, INSECT						MUSHI
MAN, PERSON						HITO
CHILD						KO
EYE						ME

WATER						MIZU

WATER   水   MIZU

RIVER   川   KAWA

FIRE   火   HI

TREE   木   KI

BIRD   鳥   TORI

HORSE   馬   UMA

COW   牛   USHI

DOG   犬   INU

FISH   魚   SAKANA

A smaller number of kanji developed not from pictures as such, but from marks indicating meaning in a more abstract way. The numbers (given later) are good examples, as also are the following:

UP, ON   上   UE
DOWN, UNDER   下   SHITA

I have only given one reading or pronunciation

each for the above kanji but actually they can be used for writing several words connected with the general ideas of "UP" or "DOWN" respectively. To give but one example, 下 may be used for writing KUDASAI: 下さい (KUDA-SA-I) meaning PLEASE, or perhaps more literally CON*DE-SCEND* TO. But to know the basic meaning is perhaps as useful as all the other things put together.

More complicated kanji were gradually built up from the simple ones. For example 木 (KI, meaning TREE) gave rise to:

COPSE, GROVE 林 HAYASHI

FOREST 森 MORI

Combined with other elements 木 gave rise to a host of kanji for things connected with wood, though the connections are not always easy to see by now. It was also used to form kanji for the names of particular trees, such as:

PINE	松 MATSU	PEAR	梨 NASHI
PEACH	桃 MOMO	MULBERRY	桑 KUWA
PLUM	梅 UME	WILLOW	柳 YANAGI
CHERRY	桜 SAKURA	JAPANESE CRYPTOMERIA	杉 SUGI

Another interesting example is the kanji for island which can still often be seen in its older form as well as in a simplified modern form:

ISLAND 嶋 島 SHIMA

The one on the left is the older form, which clearly

shows the combination of 山 (YAMA, MOUNTAIN) and 鳥 (TORI, BIRD). It is said that an island was thought of as a protruding mountain on which the birds could alight. In the simplified form the mountain has been moved to the place where the bird's legs were.

Though the great majority of kanji were first made in China, a few were thought up in Japan too, and I have chosen one of the latter as a final example. You can see for yourself how suitably designed it is:

MOUNTAIN PASS 峠 TŌGE

日 本

Perhaps this is the first Japanese word which foreigners learn, the name of the country.

NIHON or NIPPON? Both forms are used, but perhaps NIPPON is a little more solemn and dignified. The kanji do not change, whichever way they are pronounced.

The first kanji means SUN, and the second means BASIS or ORIGIN. Hence comes the well known English phrase THE LAND OF THE RISING SUN.

These kanji are to be seen everywhere. Next time you are out and about, count up how many times you can spot them.

Note that they may be written in widely differing styles in different places. But any bewilderment caused by this will pass away very quickly.

This page gives an example of how to pick out complicated kanji without getting in too much of a stew about it.

Some kanji are very simple, having only two or three strokes. Others in daily use have up to twenty-five strokes. We cannot measure the relative difficulty of kanji just by the number of strokes with which they are written, but complicated ones are admittedly more difficult to pick out at first.

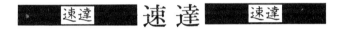

The above kanji, which are pronounced SOKU-TATSU, look rather terrifying if you stare at them in blank panic. SOKUTATSU means EXPRESS, i.e. EXPRESS MAIL.

If you see those kanji stamped in red on an envelope you will be able to appreciate that a friend or a business acquaintance has taken the trouble to send you some information you need by express mail. It is also useful to be able to recognise them in a post office, because otherwise you might wait ten minutes in a queue for counter number two only to be told at the end that you have to go to counter number four.

There is one thing about those kanji which is identical in each. It is the squiggly bit which encloses the rest:

之

And conveniently enough, just in the two places I mentioned, you are most unlikely to see two other kanji together with that same brotherly squiggly bit. If you spot two kanji like that, there, you can be 99% certain that you are looking at the Japanese for EXPRESS (MAIL).

The best way of beginning to pick out kanji of more than a few strokes is to pick out something striking about them, and, in the relevant context, look out for that. The more you come across them, the more you will get used to the parts which strike you less clearly, the parts which seem to be something of a jumble.

Thus, while being practically helpful, this approach is also a step towards the ideal. The ideal is to be able to take in the whole of a kanji with full clarity of all its parts, at a glance, and without thinking about it. This is not as difficult as it sounds, though practice helps. Try it on a train. Look at a simple kanji, (whether you understand it or not is irrelevant), then close your eyes and try to conjure up a mental image of it. Then try another, still a simple one, but one with two separate parts to it. See if you can hold them together in your mind.

五　　NUMBERS　　V

The numbers are very useful for reading dates, prices, addresses and so on. Of course many of these may be given in romanised form, but what about less well advertised exhibitions, concerts, meetings and social occasions? Such events, which some Japanese might consider to be rather off the beaten track for foreigners, could turn out to be among your most interesting and valuable experiences in Japan. It is very useful to be able to check times and places independently, and a knowledge of numerals is a basic requirement for this.

The numbers up to ten all have rather simple forms and are easily learned.

ONE	一	ICHI
TWO	二	NI
THREE	三	SAN
FOUR	四	SHI (or YON)
FIVE	五	GO
SIX	六	ROKU
SEVEN	七	SHICHI
EIGHT	八	HACHI
NINE	九	KYŪ
TEN	十	JŪ

There are other ways of reading and writing these numerals, and these are given later under SHOPS. For the moment however the main thing is to see how these simple components are built up into larger numbers. In fact they are simply strung together in a quite logical way, as in these examples.

ELEVEN	十一	JŪ-ICHI
TWELVE	十二	JŪ-NI
SIXTEEN	十六	JŪ-ROKU
NINETEEN	十九	JŪ-KYŪ
TWENTY	二十	NI-JŪ
TWENTY ONE	二十一	NI-JŪ-ICHI
TWENTY EIGHT	二十八	NI-JŪ-HACHI
THIRTY	三十	SAN-JŪ
THIRTY FIVE	三十五	SAN-JŪ-GO
FORTY	四十	YON-JŪ

Why not work out the following ones for practice?

十三	二十三	五十五	八十六
十四	三十二	五十三	九十五
八十四	七十三	六十一	六十九

Three more important units are 100, 1000, and the special 10,000.

ONE HUNDRED	百	HYAKU
ONE THOUSAND	千	SEN
TEN THOUSAND	一万	ICHI-MAN

The last of these in theory also can be given by itself, as 万, but in practice it is usual to enumerate it as "one" ten-thousand. Combinations continue as before, e.g.

2534　二千五百三十四
NI-SEN-GO-HYAKU-SAN-JŪ-YON

There are just a handful of irregularities. SEVEN is usually read as NANA (rather than SHICHI) in combination with HYAKU and SEN. There are also a few sound changes:

三百	SAN-BYAKU (more like SAM-BYAKU)	一千	IS-SEN
六百	ROP-PYAKU	三千	SAN-ZEN
八百	HAP-PYAKU	八千	HAS-SEN

The horizontal and vertical lines of some of the numerals suggest an easy cumulative arithmetic of strokes. This feature has led to some unorthodox but well-beloved kanji. After all, if

十 is TEN
卄 is nice for TWENTY, and
卅 is nice for THIRTY.

Alas, such numerals can also be amended easily by the unscrupulous. For example,

一 can easily turn into 二 or 十 and
十 can easily turn into 卄 or 卅

To prevent this, cautious financiers use alternatives so complex that they cannot be tampered with:

for 一 ICHI is used 壱 or originally 壹
for 二 NI is used 弐 or originally 貳
for 三 SAN is used 参 and

for 十 JŪ is used 拾 so that TWENTY
would be 二拾 or 弍拾

You will notice that the special forms for ONE, TWO and THREE have the appropriate horizontal strokes somewhere within them, at least originally. You might be able to pick out these special forms on old money or stamps, but now they are mainly used for handwritten amounts. For numerals in prices, see below under SHOPS.

Another of the few convenient things about the Japanese language is that the months have no special name. They are simply referred to by number.

MARCH, for example, is SAN-GATSU ("THREE-MOON"), written like this:

3月   or   三月

NOVEMBER is JŪ-ICHI-GATSU:

11月   or   十一月

Since the day of the month is also given by figures, dates are not difficult to recognise (leaving aside the rather more tricky business of how to read them aloud). Try this one, month first, then day of the month:

十一月三十日

Literally it is "ELEVEN-MOON, THIRTY-DAY", that is, NOVEMBER 30TH, or as read in Japanese, JŪ-ICHI-GATSU SAN-JŪ-NICHI.

Many exhibitions, films, festivals, etc., run for several days, and in such cases two dates are given. It is pretty obvious that the event in question runs from the earlier date to the later, but it may be useful to know that FROM and TILL are added as follows:

10月 30日から 11月 15日まで

から is read phonetically KA-RA, meaning FROM and まで is read phonetically MA-DE, meaning TILL. So the above means "From October 30th till November 15th."

Sometimes より (YO-RI) is used instead of KA-RA.

In announcements you will sometimes see something which looks familiar yet strange. You remember the kanji for NIPPON or NIHON?

日本 = Japan

You will frequently see these the other way round with the kanji for BASIS or ORIGIN in first place and that for SUN or DAY in second place. Like this:

本日

In this case it is easier to think of the first kanji as an adjective meaning something like BASIC. The meaning of the whole word is TODAY. In speech it would be read HON-JITSU; but actually a different word is usually used in conversation (KYŌ). This would be written with the kanji for NOW, as follows:

TODAY　　　　今日　KON-NICHI
　　　　　　　　　　　　(or KYŌ)

A related word is the following:

TOMORROW　明日　MYŌ-NICHI

18

The usual conversational pronunciation is ASHI-TA. The first kanji is a combination of SUN and MOON with a general meaning of BRIGHT.

DO NOT CONFUSE THIS WITH DATES!

第三回 or 才三回

read DAI-SAN-KAI. It only means THE THIRD TIME, i.e. such and such an exhibition is being held for the third time. The first kanji makes the cardinal number an ordinal (3rd), and the last has the basic meaning "going round and roung" (see its shape) and means TIME in the sense of "recurring occasion".

七 DAYS **VII**

The days of the week are often shown by one simple kanji. The seven kanji used for the seven days are as follows (with the basic meaning of each one given in brackets).

SUNDAY	日	NICHI	(SUN)
MONDAY	月	GETSU	(MOON)
TUESDAY	火	KA	(FIRE)
WEDNESDAY	水	SUI	(WATER)
THURSDAY	木	MOKU	(TREE, WOOD)
FRIDAY	金	KIN	(METAL, GOLD, MONEY)
SATURDAY	土	DO	(EARTH)

Sometimes two more kanji are added to these basic ones, but they are invariable and simply mean DAY OF THE WEEK. For example:

WEDNESDAY	水曜日	SUI-YŌ-BI
SUNDAY	日曜日	NICHI-YŌ-BI

It is quite unnecessary to rack one's brains over the details of the middle one. It is the first of the three which is important for practical purposes. Note however that the first and third kanji in the last example given are the same; two different pronunciations are used for the same kanji.

年

Above is the kanji for YEAR. In dates it is read NEN. The western calendar is widely used in Japan, but the Japanese reckoning remains important as the one in which Japanese people actually think in many contexts. It is also often seen printed.

The Japanese reckoning splits up time according to the reign of Emperors, and each of these periods has a name.

The period beginning in 1926 and current at the time of writing is called SHŌWA, written:

昭和　SHŌ-WA

and therefore the year 1976 is written out as

昭和 51 年　SHŌ-WA-GO-JŪ-ICHI-NEN

To convert a Shōwa Period date into the western calendar, add 25. To convert back, subtract 25. The two preceding periods were:

(1868–1912)　明治　MEI-JI
(1912–1926)　大正　TAI-SHŌ

The first year of any reign is written with a special kanji meaning ORIGIN or INCEPTION, and pronounced GAN. Thus the first year of the Meiji Period (1868) is written:

明治元年　MEI-JI GAN-NEN

時

The above kanji means TIME (TOKI) or HOUR (JI).

分

The above means MINUTE. The basic reading is FUN but it is usually BUN or PUN in practice when it is joined with the numbers.

Times are written like this:

THREE TWENTY 三時二十分 SAN-JI
NI-JIP-PUN

A.M. and P.M. are sometimes written in Roman letters as in English, but the following kanji are commonly used:

A.M.	午前	GO-ZEN
P.M.	午後	GO-GO

An alternative for P.M. is

P.M.	午后	GO-GO

In the above three cases, the first kanji means NOON and the second ones mean BEFORE and AFTER respectively.

The half hours may make use of a special kanji meaning HALF:

HALF 半 HAN

and using this, HALF PAST TEN, for example, is simply written as

HALF PAST TEN 十時半 JŪ-JI-HAN

There is no special kanji for the quarters which are expressed as 15 or 45 minutes.

FIVE FIFTEEN 5時15分 GO-JI JŪ-GO-FUN
THREE FORTY-FIVE

3時45分

SAN-JI YON-JŪ-GO-FUN

You probably remember this kanji from the introduction to this book:

RAIN 雨 AME

It is used as the top part of other kanji connected with the weather. For example, the character for SNOW is that for rain with a hand drawn beneath, because one of the characteristics of snow is that you can pick it up.

SNOW 雪 YUKI

Another similar one means THUNDER. The bottom part looks very solid. As a matter of fact it means RICE-FIELD, so that the idea of thunder is given by rain over the rice-fields.

THUNDER 雷 KAMINARI

Adding a vicious forked tail we have what used to be the character for LIGHTNING

電 (DEN)

It is now no longer used for lightning as such, but by a transfer of meaning it signifies ELECTRICITY, first and foremost in the compound word DEN-KI, and then in several other common words:

ELECTRICITY	電気	DEN-KI
TELEGRAM	電報	DEN-PŌ
TELEPHONE	電話	DEN-WA

(In this last case the second character means TO SPEAK, the left hand part of it being WORD and the right hand part being TONGUE.)

ELECTRIC TRAIN or TRAM, STREETCAR	電車	DEN-SHA

(The second character of this term is used for all kinds of vehicles.)

Tram networks in large cities such as Kyōto are usually known as "city electric":

TRAM (Network), CITY STREETCARS	市電	SHI-DEN

十一　　　　　　　　　　XI

STATIONS (EXITS AND ENTRANCES)

Stations in Japan are often large and complicated, especially when different railway companies use the same station. Moreover they sometimes change their shape and have temporary passages and exits.

The kanji for MOUTH was given earlier:

MOUTH　　　　　　口　　　　　KUCHI

Combined with another, it means

ENTRANCE　　　　入口　　　IRI-GUCHI

and with another, it means

EXIT　　　　　　出口　　　DEGUCHI

Sometimes you may see both together as

出入口　DE-IRI-GUCHI

and this means that you can go in or out.

A very special exit is the emergency exit, usually marked by a sign in green characters:

EMERGENCY EXIT　非常口　HI-JŌ-GUCHI

Nowadays there seems to be a trend in some buildings to make the ordinary exit the best one to use in emergencies as well and so one sees a sign which combines DEGUCHI with HI-JŌ-GU-CHI, thus

非常出口　HI-JŌ-DE-GUCHI

This portmanteau term includes reference to the ordinary exit which you are probably seeking.

Some entrances and exits are obvious anyway, but in large stations you may easily follow the crowd and end up not out in the street, but getting into another train. Of course it is useful to spot exit and entrance signs in other places as well as in stations.

Large stations sometimes have several exits to different places. A famous one is the exit to the eastern side of Tokyo Station, known as

八重州口　YA-E-SU-GUCHI

The passage across to the Yaesu-guchi from the other side is very hard to find unless you can spot these characters above its entrance. The western side of Tokyo Station is known as

丸ノ内　　MARU-NO-UCHI

Station exits are often marked according to the points of the compass, which are:

NORTH　北　KITA

WEST　西　NISHI　　　EAST　東　HIGASHI

SOUTH　南　MINAMI

When the word KUCHI is added on to the end of

these, it becomes -GUCHI, as in DEGUCHI (above), thus also:

北 口
KITA-GUCHI

西 口   東 口
NISHI-GUCHI   HIGASHI-GUCHI

南 口
MINAMI-GUCHI

These of course mean NORTH ENTRANCE (or EXIT), etc. The points of the compass are also often used in place names, and especially in the names of two or more different stations serving one place. Between the cardinal points lies the centre:

CENTRAL EXIT   中央口   CHŪ-Ō-GUCHI

The first two kanji here both mean CENTRE, and in combination they just mean more obviously CENTRE.

One other kind of ENTRANCE found in every station is the:

TICKET CONTROL 改札口 KAI-SATSU-GUCHI

This is the entrance to the platforms, where tickets are snipped.

十二   XII

STATIONS (TICKETS AND PLATFORMS)

To buy a ticket you have to find the ticket office, and if you can spot the sign for it, it may save walking right round the station. It may be written in kanji, but often is just in HIRAGANA, so look for either.

TICKET OFFICE   切符売場   KIPPU-URIBA

TICKET OFFICE きっぷうりば KIPPU-URIBA

The ordinary conversational word for TICKET is KIPPU, but there are many different kinds of ticket which may be sold at different windows. The words for all of these end in

(-TICKET)   券   (-KEN)

The names of these special tickets are admittedly not easy to learn quickly, but if you just want an ordinary ticket, it might be worth gambling on *not* waiting in a long queue where a long list of these is posted! If the queue you are in seems to get stuck, the answer is to pull this book out of your pocket and see if you can work out where you are heading for!

定 期 券 TEI-KI-KEN	This is a big ticket with which you can travel as often as you like on the stretch indicated for one month, three months, etc.

回 数 券 KAI-SŪ-KEN	This is a whole strip of ordinary tickets bought at a cheaper rate and to be used within a certain time.
特 急 券 TOK-KYŪ-KEN	EXPRESS TICKETS
グ リ ー ン券 GU-RII-N-KEN	GREEN TICKETS For special amenity travel, as opposed to the ordinary class.
団 体 券 DAN-TAI-KEN	GROUP TICKETS
指定席券 SHI-TEI-SEKI-KEN	RESERVED SEAT TICKETS
寝 台 券 SHIN-DAI-KEN	SLEEPER TICKETS
入 場 券 NYŪ-JŌ-KEN	PLATFORM TICKETS Literally this just means ENTRANCE TICKET. The middle kanji of the three means PLACE, as in the word for TICKET OFFICE given above which literally means TICKET SELLING PLACE.

Notice the term for SEAT which may also be useful inside the train, usually seats to avoid, so that one does not need to suffer the embarrassment of being turned out of them:

GREEN SEATS	グ リ ー ン席	GU-RII-N SEKI
GROUP SEATS	団 体 席	DAN-TAI-SEKI
RESERVED SEATS	指 定 席	SHI-TEI-SEKI

Two more practical points about buying tickets. Firstly different train lines and even different batches of destinations are sometimes separated out from one another, so it is often a help if you can get to know the kanji for the places to which you go or the lines which you most use. Secondly, since the late 1960's tickets for shorter journeys are now sold almost exclusively from automatic machines. This has led to a new problem for foreigners because the maps showing the prices required for various destinations give the names of all the stations in kanji. Since one cannot talk to the machine and hope for the best, the only way is to note the name of your destination in kanji, seizing if possible on some idiosyncrasy, and to get familiar as quickly as possible with its approximate location relative to other known stations. It can then be picked out on the map.

Having bought your ticket the next thing is to go to the right platform. Platforms are often numbered like this:

PLATFORM NO. 3	3 番ホーム	SAN-BAN-FŌ-MU

BAN means NUMBER (NO.). FŌMU (ホーム) should strictly be romanised as HŌMU, but I used the F above to show that it represents FORM, short for the English word PLATFORM. F and H are not really distinct in pronunciation. Compare FUJI-SAN, which sometimes comes out in speech rather as HUJI-SAN. Note also that the final U of MU is present because Japanese words must end either in a vowel or in N. The word could be privately rewritten as FORMu or HORMu, showing the diminutive stature of the "u" on the end.

Sometimes, instead of FŌMU, we find the kanji 線 which means LINE. You may remember that the left hand part of it means THREAD.

LINE NO. FIVE　　五番線　　GO-BAN-SEN

If you have learnt the name of the place to which you are going in Japanese you can look out for it on a hanging signboard written in kanji, though romanised versions are sometimes offered as well. If you do look at the kanji, you will notice that almost every train seems to go to a place called

方面　HŌ-MEN

This is not because HŌMEN is the Japanese for THE ETERNAL CITY, but simply because it means DIRECTION, or as we should put it, TO . . . .

TO TŌKYO　　　東京方面　TŌ-KYŌ-HŌ-MEN

Instead of HŌMEN, you may also see YUKI, which means literally GOING (TO) . . .

TO KYŌTO　　　京都行き　KYŌ-TO-YUKI
TO ŌSAKA　　　大阪ゆき　Ō-SAKA-YUKI

列 車
RES-SHA

This is the simple word for TRAIN. Literally it means a ROW OF WAGONS, RETSU (the first kanji) meaning a ROW and SHA meaning VEHICLE, CARRIAGE or WAGON.

汽 車
KI-SHA

KI means STEAM and so KI-SHA means a STEAM TRAIN.

電 車
DEN-SHA

ELECTRIC TRAIN (in other contexts TRAM or STREET-CAR).

Now come some words of great practical importance which can save you from wasting a great deal of time or from being carried far past the station where you wanted to get out.

各駅停車
KAKU-EKI-TEI-SHA

A train which stops at every station. EACH-STATION-STOP-TRAIN.

普通列車
FU-TSŪ-RES-SHA

Or FUTSŪ-DENSHA (普通電車). ORDINARY TRAIN. In practice this is the same as the above.

準 急
JUN-KYŪ

The words DENSHA or RES-SHA may be added to this. Usually translated SEMI-EX-PRESS, this train misses out some small stations, especially near the point of departure.

快速電車 KAI-SOKU-DEN- SHA	FAST TRAIN. This is really the same as a JUNKYŪ, but the words vary from line to line.
急 行 KYŪ-KŌ	The words DENSHA or RES-SHA may be added. Literally it means HURRY-GO (compare 行き YUKI on an earlier page). EXPRESS.
特 急 TOK-KYŪ	TOKU (here TOK) means SPECIAL. SPECIAL EXPRESS.
超 特 急 CHŌ-TOK-KYŪ	SUPER SPECIAL EXPRESS. These really go places.

The various lines or routes each have their own name, but before giving a few examples it will be well to look at the kanji for NATIONAL RAILWAYS:

NATIONAL
    RAILWAYS   国鉄   KOKU-TETSU

The first kanji, KOKU, means COUNTRY or NATIONAL. TETSU, the second, means IRON, being an abbreviation in the present case for TETSU-DŌ (鉄道) IRON ROAD. Notice that the left hand part (金) means METAL.

In some stations a particular line may be called the NATIONAL RAILWAY LINE, in contrast to some other line belonging to a private company:

NATIONAL
    RAILWAY LINE   国鉄線 KOKU-TETSU-SEN

There now follow the names of a few well known lines in the Tokyo area which belong to the national railways:

山手線 YAMA-TE-SEN

This is the loop line which runs all round Tokyo. YAMA means MOUNTAIN and TE means HAND; but YAMATE means BLUFF, (the Concise Oxford Dictionary explains this as a "headland with perpendicular broad face"), allegedly referring to the hilly section of Tokyo.

中央線 CHŪ-Ō-SEN

CHŪŌ means CENTRAL as in CHŪŌGUCHI (中央口 CENTRAL EXIT or ENTRANCE) given earlier. This line runs across the centre of Tokyo.

京浜東北線 KEI-HIN-TŌ-HOKU-SEN

KEI is an abbreviation for TŌKYŌ (東京) and HIN for YOKOHAMA (横浜). TŌHOKU means NORTH-EAST, in this case referring to the north-east of the Tokyo area.

新幹線 SHIN-KAN-SEN

This is the NEW TRUNK LINE, the super express line from Tokyo to Nagoya, Kyōto, Ōsaka, and now down as far as Hakata.

地下鉄(線) CHI-KA-TETSU(-SEN)

This is the underground railway run by a metropolitan authority (it is not a national railway). CHI means EARTH, KA means UNDER and TETSU is short for RAILROAD as explained above.

Finally here are two tickets to puzzle out:

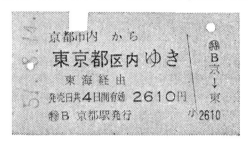

The first ticket is for travel from Kyōto to any station in the Tokyo area. The second is used in conjunction with it for travel on the Shinkansen. Some new kanji: 市 SHI, CITY; 区 KU, AREA; 内 NAI, WTHIN; 円 EN, YEN; 駅 EKI, STATION.
東海経由 TŌ-KAI-KEI-YU, EASTERN SEA ROUTE;
4日間有効 YOK-KA-KAN-YŪ-KŌ, FOUR DAYS VALID;
途中出場できません TO-CHŪ-SHUTSU-JŌ-DEKIMASEN, BREAK IN JOURNEY NOT ALLOWED; 自由席 JI-YŪ-SEKI, "FREE", i.e. NON-RESERVED SEAT.

TOBACCO AND TELEPHONES

If you want a telephone, find a tobacconist. Most of the little tobacco booths dotted about here and there also have a public telephone. And of course smokers find tobacco booths attractive in their own right. You can easily spot these at a distance by the standard sign illustrated below. It is sometimes, but not always, oval in shape and has three white HIRAGANA symbols on a red background.

たばこ   TA-BA-KO

Next time you walk down the street, see how many times you can spot it. After seeing a few, three of the HIRAGANA symbols will be inalienably yours.

十五　FLOORS OR STOREYS　XV

Major department stores have a plan in English just inside the entrance, and having discovered at which floor one wants to shop it is an easy matter to find that floor since the numerals are usually Arabic.

But this is *not* the case in all tall buildings, and knowledge of the Japanese numerals is very useful for getting about them quickly.

The kanji which follows the number of each floor is:

STOREY (FLOOR)　　階　KAI

It is used like this:

FIRST FLOOR (English GROUND FLOOR)	一階	IK-KAI
SECOND FLOOR (English 1st FLOOR)	二階	NI-KAI

The English system for numbering floors is at loggerheads with the Japanese and American throughout.

One more word of warning is necessary before giving a complete table. The kanji for GROUND, 地, occurs in two other places in this little book, and the reader might make an intelligent guess at:

地 階 CHI-KAI

This means however not "ground floor" but BASE-MENT. Another word for BASEMENT is CHIKA

十四   XIV

(compare CHIKATETSU):

BASEMENT 地下 CHI-KA

Now a whole building can be shown:

ROOF-TOP 屋上 OKU-JŌ

10th FLOOR	十階	JIK-KAI
9th FLOOR	九階	KYŪ-KAI
8th FLOOR	八階	HACHI-KAI
7th FLOOR	七階	NANA-KAI
6th FLOOR	六階	ROK-KAI
5th FLOOR	五階	GO-KAI
4th FLOOR	四階	YON-KAI
3rd FLOOR	三階	SAN-GAI
2nd FLOOR	二階	NI-KAI
1st FLOOR	一階	IK-KAI

車車　　　　　　　　　　　　　　　　　木 林

BASEMENT 1	地下一階	CHI-KA-IK-KAI
BASEMENT 2	地下二階	CHI-KA-NI-KAI
BASEMENT 3	地下三階	CHI-KA-SAN-GAI

N. B. Cars and trees are shown at street level. Turn the cars: 車車 and you have 車 KURUMA, a Japanese word for MOTOR-CAR (AUTOMOBILE). You may remember that it is the same kanji as the SHA of DENSHA (電車).

十六　　SHOPS　　XVI

In spite of the anxiety of some of our Japanese friends on our behalf, shopping in Japan is not a great problem. Most of the wares offered are clearly displayed and it is highly probable that if you can't see it they haven't got it. Prices too are usually well marked. It probably does not take anybody too long to realise that

円　means YEN,

usually pronounced more like EN in Japanese.

But assuming that, perhaps with the help of the Japanese numerals, one knows the price, the problem may remain in some shops of how much one gets for the price. If one is staying a couple of days in a port town, soon to leave the country, a hit and miss method about the price of a few apples or peaches doesn't matter. But if one is staying longer it becomes very useful to know if the price marked is the price of three apples or five apples. In this respect the following kanji is important:

PIECE, ITEM (German: Stück)	個	KO
ONE (i.e. one apple, etc.)	一個	IK-KO
ONE (FOR) 　FIFTY YEN	一個五十円	IK-KO GO-JŪ-EN
TWO (FOR) 　80 YEN	二個八十円	NI-KO HACHI-JŪ-EN
FOUR (FOR) 150 YEN	四個百五十円	YON-KO HYAKU- GO-JŪ-EN

In place of this counting kanji may be used a simple numeral, but if so the numeral is read not with the shorter reading imported from China (given above under NUMBERS), but with the longer native Japanese word. The phonetic symbol TSU つ must usually be added, and sometimes the KA-TAKANA form ツ is used for emphasis. The native Japanese readings only exist for the numbers ONE to TEN, and are as follows:

ONE	一つ	HITO-TSU
TWO	二つ	FUTA-TSU
THREE	三つ	MIT-TSU
FOUR	四つ	YO-TSU (or YOT-TSU)
FIVE	五つ	ITSU-TSU
SIX	六つ	MU-TSU (or MUT-TSU)
SEVEN	七つ	NANA-TSU
EIGHT	八つ	YA-TSU (or YAT-TSU)
NINE	九つ	KOKONO-TSU
TEN	十	TŌ

To illustrate, two of the examples given just above are repeated in this alternative form, and written vertically (so read right to left):

一
五 つ
十
円

HITO-TSU
GO-JŪ-EN

百 四
五 つ
十
円

YO-TSU
HYAKU-GO-JŪ-EN

Ripe fruit and vegetables are often put out at bargain prices to be sold by the dish.

ONE DISH 200 YEN	一皿二百円	HITO-SARA NI-HYAKU-EN

or, as it is sometimes put to make it seem even more,

ONE MOUN- TAIN 300 YEN	一山三百円	HITO-YAMA SAN-BYAKU-EN

The character 本 (HON) has already been given above in the word 日本 (NI-HON or NIPPON). Another use of this versatile kanji is as a numerative for cylindrical objects, and so it is often used for carrots, cucumbers, etc.

ONE FOR 50 YEN	一本五十円	IP-PON GO-JŪ-YEN

It will be noticed that while the basic reading is HON, this pronunciation may be altered in compounds. The written message can however be understood without detailed knowledge of such intricacies.

Weight is usually measured in kilograms, abbreviated to KIRO and written in KATAKANA:

KILOGRAM	キロ	KIRO

Numbers are simply prefixed to it:

ONE KILOGRAM	一キロ	ICHI-KIRO

It must be admitted that many shopkeepers use Arabic numerals for marking up prices nowadays, but there is no standard rule on this and good custom dies hard. Unfortunately even the high prices given in the examples are likely to be antiquated all too soon!

Food is very complicated, but so important and enjoyable that some introductory help must be given here. Of first importance are the signs outside restaurants indicating the type of food served. One common term in these is that for cooking in general:

CUISINE　料 理　RYŌ-RI

The signs are often written vertically, so here are four kinds of CUISINE side by side, numbered to link up with the explanations below.

日本料理	中華料理	朝鮮料理	西洋料理
1	2	3	4

1. NI-HON-RYŌ-RI, JAPANESE COOKING.
2. CHŪ-KA-RYŌ-RI, CHINESE COOKING. The name CHŪ-KA was traditionally given to China (by the Chinese), CHŪ meaning MIDDLE and KA meaning ELEGANT or BRILLIANT. Nowadays CHINA is more regularly known as

CHŪ-GOKU　中 国　CHINA

3. CHŌ-SEN-RYŌ-RI, KOREAN COOKING. Less common than the other types, but to be recommended. Also KAN-KOKU-RYŌ-RI 韓国料理:

KANKOKU of course means KOREA, the KOKU being the same as the -GOKU of CHŪ-GOKU above.

4. SEI-YŌ-RYŌ-RI, WESTERN COOKING. The first kanji means WEST, and is otherwise pronounced NISHI as in NISHI-GUCHI given earlier. SEI-YŌ is the normal term for WESTERN-STYLE.

Other signs outside restaurants indicate particular types of dish rather than the civilisation of origin, and a group of these which follows will introduce some of the best known dishes.

お そ ば	中 華 そ ば	焼 そ ば	す き 焼	焼 鳥	天 ぷ ら	寿 司	軽 食
1	2	3	4	5	6	7	8

1. O-SOBA. The O is honorific. SOBA is a thin yellowish noodle served in many different ways.

2. CHŪ-KA-SOBA. CHINESE SOBA, served with chopped meat and vegetables and finely seasoned.

3. YAKI-SOBA. FRIED SOBA. This term is sometimes written in HIRAGANA throughout: や きそば.

4. SUKI-YAKI. Known even to foreigners as SUKIYAKI, and the one dish which the Japanese *expect* us to like. It may also be seen in HIRA-GANA only: すきやき.

5. YAKI-TORI. ROAST CHICKEN, usually in pieces on sticks, also often written in HIRAGA-NA: やきとり.

6. TEN-PU-RA. Best known as TEMPURA

(equal stress on each syllable please!) consisting of pieces of vegetable or little fish or prawns fried with batter in deep fat.

7. SU-SHI. Best known as SUSHI, though it usually takes an honorific in speech if not always in writing: O-SUSHI. Delicacies of raw fish on wads of rice, mouth-watering even just to think of in retrospect, but expensive.

8. KEI-SHOKU. LIGHT FOOD, i.e. various snack meals from among further examples to follow below. The second kanji of this term is also found in the following very useful word:

FIXED MENU 定 食 TEI-SHOKU

If you are unadventurous or indecisive, just walk in and ask for TEI-SHOKU and you will be given a set meal at an average price. Not all restaurants offer a TEI-SHOKU however, and so there follow examples of more specific dishes.

The various kinds of restaurant listed above offer meals at all prices, but there are thousands of little restaurants all over Japan which sell mainly noodles or simple rice dishes. These are the kind to dive into for a quick cheap lunch. It is common practice to put plastic models of the main dishes in a window, with the price. The only difficulty, for the discreet foreigner, is deciding how to pronounce the name written beside the price of the dish which you select. There are unfortunately numerous variations, and these will usually be written on strips of paper pinned to the wall inside the shop. Some of the more common kinds fall into the two main groups of rice dishes and noodle dishes.

If you are looking for solid food based on rice, a useful kanji is:

丼　DONBURI (or just DON, sounding more like DOM)

A DONBURI is a bowl of rice with something on top as in the following.

玉子丼	親子丼	カツ丼	天丼	中華丼
1	2	3	4	5

1. TAMA-GO-DONBURI. TAMAGO means EGG. The word TAMAGO usually has its own special kanji: (卵), but in this case it is made up by borrowing the sounds of two quite different ones: TAMA, meaning BALL or PRECIOUS STONE, and KO (here becoming GO), meaning CHILD.

2. OYA-KO-DONBURI. OYA means PARENT and KO means CHILD. The PARENT appears in the form of bits of chicken meat, while the CHILD, of course, is the EGG.

3. KA-TSU-DONBURI. KATSU is a corruption of CUTLET, and in practice means a small piece of rather fatty meat wrapped up in batter. As a general rule, the quality of the meat fits the appearance of the restaurant, but one can go sadly astray here. Since KATSU represents a loan-

word from English it is usually written in KATA-KANA syllables.

4. TEN-DON. TEN is short for TENPURA (see above), and in the case of TEMPURA DONBURI, the TEMPURA part usually consists of a couple of large prawns.

5. CHŪ-KA-DONBURI. CHŪ-KA means CHINESE, as before, and this dish is meat and vegetables in a sauce, placed on top of a bowl of rice. Here are some more DOMBURIS.

海	た	か	カ
老	ぬ	つ	レ
天	き		―
丼	丼	丼	丼
1	2	3	4

1. E-BI-TEN-DON. PRAWN TENPURA DONBURI. This is what TEN-DON usually is anyway. EBI written as shown is quite irregular phonetically. The first kanji means SEA and the second means OLD.

2. TA-NU-KI DONBURI. BADGER DONBURI. A good way to discover what this is would be to have some.

3. KA-TSU-DON. CUTLET DONBURI, as before. This time it is given in HIRAGANA, to illustrate that restaurant proprietors are very haphazard about their choice between HIRAGANA and KATAKANA. This untidiness is reflected again in later examples to save repeating everything.

4. KA-REE DONBURI. CURRY DONBURI, like

CURRY RICE (below) but served in a bowl instead of sprawled across a plate.

Another popular way of eating rice is fried, with decorative additions. The basic form is

FRIED RICE 焼めし or 焼飯 YAKI-MESHI

Inevitable variants appear such as

玉子焼飯 TAMA-GO-YAKI-MESHI
　　　　　EGG AND FRIED RICE

海老焼飯 E-BI-YAKI-MESHI
　　　　　PRAWN AND FRIED RICE

五目やきめし GO-MOKU-YAKI-MESHI
　　　　　FIVE-EYED FRIED RICE

Please return to the latter when you have discovered what FIVE-EYED SOBA is.

Other rice dishes are semi-westernised and written in KATAKANA, e.g.

カレーライス KA-REE RAISU, CURRY RICE
　(rice with curried indefinables on it)

オムライス OMU RAISU, OM RICE
　(OMU is short for オムレツ OMURETSU, meaning OMELETTE, thus OMELETTE RICE)

チキンライス CHIKIN RAISU
　(fried rice with little pieces of chicken)

カツライス KATSU RAISU
　(CUTLET RICE, but see note on KATSU DON above)

Sometimes these rice dishes are given in menus in romanised form, but in this case the occasional FLY RICE or FRIED LICE are simply good old

FRIED RICE.

The other main family of dishes is the noodle family. There must be hundreds of variations on the noodle, and those which boast the status of local specialities are especially well worth trying. The following terms are examples of the ubiquitous.

う	ヤ	肉	五	ラ
ど	キ	ソ	目	ー
	ソ		ソ	メ
ん	バ	バ	バ	ン
1	2	3	4	5

1. U-DO-N. UDON is rather different from the other noodles mentioned here, being thick, white and soft. It is usually served with a few bits of meat and onion on top to give flavour (needed).

2. YA-KI-SO-BA. FRIED SOBA. This was given above in slightly different form among the signs found outside restaurants. SOBA is the thinner, yellowish noodle, usually served with something just to go with it.

3. NIKU-SO-BA. This is SOBA with a little MEAT with it, NIKU meaning MEAT.

4. GO-MOKU-SO-BA. GOMOKU means FIVE EYES, so this might be called FIVE-EYED SOBA. The FIVE EYES are supposed to be five different things put in with the noodles, but when you have eaten it many times without ever being quite able to puzzle out what the five are, you realise that it is just a fancy name for "various", not to say "miscellaneous".

5. RĀ-ME-N. This is the cheapest and most

everyday dish of which the name ends in MEN,
see below, but it is not to be despised. Just slurp
it down.

The MEN of RĀMEN is usually written phonetically in KATAKANA, but it is also the generic
term for noodle dishes. As a heading in menus,
this term in full is:

NOODLES　　麵 類　　MEN-RUI

The right hand part of the kanji for MEN is the
same as the MEN of HŌMEN (方面) in Section
XII. The left hand part gives the meaning of
WHEAT (or BARLEY, etc.) and by itself would
be pronounced MUGI. The bottom of the left hand
part is sometimes extended with a wonderful
flourish in a whole row of items posted on the
wall, thus:

⋮	⋮	什景炒麺	天津麺	広東麺	鶏糸湯麺	肉糸湯麺	什景湯麺
炒麺	炒麺						

...which means that there are noodles about.

Many smaller restaurants do just a few dishes
in "Chinese" or in "western" style, so that in one
place you may find both 中華そば and カツライス.
Here and there however is a restaurant which
specialises in the Chinese dishes, some of which are
particularly common, tasty and filling.

酢ぶた SU-BU-TA.

SUBUTA could be rendered VINEGARED PORK,

as SU is VINEGAR and BUTA is PORK (or indeed as a matter of fact PIG).

酢ぶたランチ SU-BU-TA RA-N-CHI.
SUBUTA LUNCH is the above with soup etc. added.

中華ランチ CHŪ-KA-RA-N-CHI.
CHINESE LUNCH, a small cluster of servings, the main one being meat and vegetables in sauce.

甘煮 UMA-NI.
Literally, SWEET-BOILING, being meat and vegetables boiled in thick soya sauce with some sugar. Sometimes it is written just うまに or うま煮.

肉うま煮 NIKU-UMANI.
MEAT UMANI, including more distinct pieces of meat.

野菜うまに YA-SAI-UMANI.
VEGETABLE UMANI, preferred by those not so eager for meat.

五目うまに GO-MOKU-UMANI.
FIVE-EYED UMANI (see above on FIVE-EYED).

えびうま煮 E-BI UMANI.
PRAWN UMANI.

とりうま煮 TORI-UMANI.
CHICKEN UMANI. And of course...

うまにランチ UMANI-RANCHI.

ワンタン WANTAN.
Flavoured pork and onion wrapped in flour-paste and served in soup.

ギョウザ GYŌZA.

Similar to above but in crescent shaped portions eaten dry with soya sauce.

Not to be confused with the kanji for VIN-EGAR given above is the important SAKE (usually O-SA-KE in conversation):

SAKE　酒　SAKE

Other drinks are rather western in origin and are given in KATAKANA which can be puzzled out. Tea (Japanese tea) is not listed on the menu because you get it anyway.

十八　THE POST OFFICE XVIII

In post offices there are usually several counters for different things, and since there are often queues it is quite useful to know which queue to stand in.

Do you remember this?

速　達

The two squiggly parts remind us that it is the Japanese for EXPRESS MAIL, SOKUTATSU.

Here are some more kanji which may come in useful in post offices as you gradually get to know them.

STAMPS	切　手	KIT-TE
REGISTERED MAIL	書　留	KAKI-TOME
PARCELS	小　包	KO-ZUTSUMI
SEAMAIL	船　便	FUNA-BIN
AIRMAIL	航空便	KŌ-KŪ-BIN

Post offices seem to be rather thinly spaced, so it is a good idea to remember where they are when you have found them. The word may be useful, though they are not extravagantly advertised.

POST OFFICE　郵便局 YŪ-BIN-KYOKU

YŪBIN means POST, and KYOKU means OFFICE. So now you can understand what is usually written on Japanese stamps:

JAPAN MAIL　日本郵便　NIP-PON YŪ-BIN

There is also a conventional sign for POST or MAIL, which is not a real kanji and therefore has no pronunciation.　It may be helpful:

十九　　BANKS　　XIX

Even if one is not actually looking for a bank their signs are useful for getting to know kanji. Many of the names are well known. Ask a friend to explain one or two and then look out for branch buildings in other places. Usually they are prosperous-looking places and have a vertical sign with four kanji. The last two kanji are always the same and mean BANK.

BANK　　　銀 行　　　GIN-KŌ

GIN means SILVER. You will notice that the left-hand part of it (金) is a kanji which you have met before meaning GOLD, METAL or MONEY.

Another bank sign which is fixed to about half the telegraph poles in Japan is:

質　　　SHICHI

The sound SHICHI also means SEVEN (written 七 however), so this bank is sometimes called the ICHI-ROKU-GINKO, the ONE-SIX BANK. It means PAWNSHOP.

二十　　THE FIRM　　**XX**

The word for FIRM is invariably translated COMPANY...

FIRM (COMPANY)　会　社　KAI-SHA

KAI means MEETING and SHA means ASSOCIATION, so the two kanji go together very nicely. A company usually writes itself up as:

株式会社 KABU-SHIKI-KAI-SHA

which means JOINT-STOCK COMPANY and is the equivalent of & CO., or INC. when found in names.

These kanji may be seen anywhere, so please look out for them on your travels. Less common is:

LTD. CO. 有限会社 YŪ-GEN-GAI-SHA

二十一　　　　　　　　**XXI**

SHRINES, TEMPLES
AND ALTERNATIVE READINGS

Here are a few words of interest which at the
same time illustrate some of the intricacies of
actually reading kanji. The casual reader will be
quite right not to worry too much about the latter.

SHRINE　　　**神 社**　　　JIN-JA

The first of the two kanji above means GOD or
GODS, usually in the traditional Japanese sense
of KAMI (another way of reading it), as found for
example in the word KAMIKAZE. You have already met the second kanji in the word KAISHA
(会社 FIRM or COMPANY). Notice that in this
case it is pronounced not SHA but JA. This is
a good example of a common procedure: the first
consonant of the second kanji in a word is often
hardened in this way.

SHINTO　　　　神 道　　　　SHIN-DŌ

You are not so likely to see this word just by
walking around, but it may be interesting to know
what lies behind the well-known word SHINTO.
The first kanji is the same as the one above, but
this time it is pronounced SHIN. The second,
which is usually pronounced MICHI or DŌ, means
ROAD, PATH or WAY. So you can see that
SHINTO, the old indigenous religion of Japan,

means THE WAY OF THE KAMI (GODS), or THE KAMI WAY.

BUDDHISM   仏 教   BUK-KYŌ

The first kanji of the above word, meaning BUD-DHA, is fundamentally pronounced either HOTO-KE or BUTSU. In this case the reading BUTSU is taken, but it is modified by the following KYŌ, as shown. KYŌ means TEACHING.

TEMPLE (Buddhist)   寺   TERA

This kanji is usually pronounced differently in the names of particular temples, where it is most often used:

浅 草 寺
ASA-KUSA-
    DERA

In the name of this famous temple in Tokyo the T is hardened to D, another example of what was mentioned above. (It is some-times read SEN-SŌ-JI)

東 大 寺
TŌ-DAI-JI

More frequently however, the kanji is pronounced JI, as in the name of the great temple in Nara shown on the left. You have met the first kanji of the name as HIGASHI (EAST). Here it is read TŌ. The middle one (DAI) means LARGE or GREAT.

大   仏
DAI-BUTSU

In the TŌDAIJI there is a great Buddha image, known in Japa-nese as the DAIBUTSU. Another famous DAIBUTSU is to be found at Kamakura.

On maps shrines are usually marked with the sign:

鳥

It is not a real kanji but it represents the gate or TORII characteristic of shrines.

Temples are usually denoted on maps by the Buddhist swastika:

卍

Note that the tails point in an anti-clockwise direction, just the opposite of the Nazi swastika. Although strictly speaking it cannot be pronounced, it is known as the MANJI. The symbol came to Japan from India, via China and Korea, along with the Buddhist religion.

Japanese is usually written vertically from top to bottom beginning on the right hand of the page, or horizontally like English running from left to right. Some old inscriptions on temple buildings and suchlike read horizontally from right to left, but they are few and far between.

Striking however is the common usage for signs painted on commercial vehicles.

THEY ARE PAINTED FROM THE FRONT TO THE BACK OF THE VEHICLE.

This means that on one side they are written from left to right and on the other side from right to left. The result is that, assuming the vehicle to be moving forwards, the signs always come into our field of vision in the right order, regardless of which side of it we are standing.

The figures below are intended to represent vehicles moving in opposite directions. Below each vehicle the kanji and KATAKANA which appear on it are given in romanised form in the same order. The syllables are retained as units even when reading from right to left, since the individual Japanese characters remain unchanged in themselves.

When you have worked them out, try it with some real vehicles.

TŌKYŌ BUS

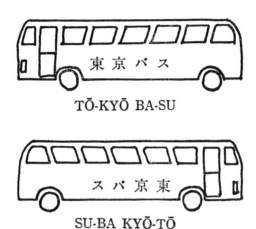

東京バス

TŌ-KYŌ BA-SU

スバ京東

SU-BA KYŌ-TŌ

TAXI

タクシー

TA-KU-SHI

ーシクタ

SHI-KU-TA

二十三　　TOILET　　XXIII

You may be surprised how often the notice for a toilet is not given in English, even in Tokyo.

Sometimes it is written up like this:

TOILT　or even　　TO LET

In Japanese the common word, equivalent to the English word "lavatory", is written like this:

LAVATORY　　便 所　　BEN-JO

(BEN is written with the same kanji as the BIN of YŪBIN meaning POST). A more refined word is the following:

TOILET　　お手洗い　　O-TE-ARAI

NB. The first character is the phonetic sign for O and is simply a word of politeness. The second means HAND. The third and fourth go together, the final phonetic symbol completing the sound of the character, ARA-I, meaning WASHING. The total result, O-TE-ARAI, means HAND-WASHING and is the answer to the English euphemism, "May I wash my hands?"

Sometimes the same word is found in the following form.

TOILET　　御手洗い　　O-TE-ARAI

This time the first character is much more complicated than the simple phonetic symbol which took its place in the first example. However the meaning and sound are the same. You may see this character in other contexts but you can always feel free to ignore it completely.

The two doors may be distinguished as follows:

MEN 男 OTOKO   WOMEN 女 ONNA

OTOKO is the usual word for MAN (MEN) as opposed to WOMAN, and ONNA is the usual word for WOMAN (WOMEN).

MEN 男子 DAN-SHI   WOMEN 女子 JO-SHI

In this case the kanji for OTOKO and ONNA are used as before, but they are read in a different way, that is, with the pronunciation which came over from China together with the kanji. The second kanji appended to each means CHILD, but the combined words DANSHI and JOSHI means not so much BOYS and GIRLS as MALE and FEMALE (for humans).

GENTLEMEN 紳士 (用) SHIN-SHI (YŌ)
LADIES   婦人 (用) FU-JIN (YŌ)

These are rather more stylish words. The kanji in brackets (YŌ) may or may not be added. It means FOR THE USE OF. If these last examples seem rather difficult, look out for the little ONNA on the left-hand side of 婦!

Or just look out for the international kanji.

二十四 ADDRESSES XXIV

Although Japanese place names are sometimes very difficult to read, postal addresses have some features in common so that we can at least know which part of an address is which. With this knowledge and a spirit of pioneering guesswork one can often put oneself in the picture when communications are otherwise at a low ebb.

Addresses always have some of the following components:

県 KEN   This is sometimes translated into English as PREFECTURE. It is similar to the French "Préfecture" or to the English COUNTY.

郡 GUN   This is a subdivision of a KEN, and could perhaps be translated RURAL DISTRICT.

市 SHI   This means CITY. Places which have the status of a city are treated independently of GUN.

区 KU   This is sometimes translated WARD, though it is doubtful whether such a translation is very useful. A KU or WARD is a section of a large city such as Tokyo or Kyoto.

町 MACHI   In country districts this means TOWN,
(or CHŌ)   but there may not be much of a town to be seen. It is often simply an area of scattered fields and buildings

	marked off as a MACHI for adminis-
	trative purposes. In a city, there
	may be several or many MACHI, and
	in large cities the MACHI or CHŌ is
	really a subdivision of a KU.
丁目 CHŌ-ME	This is a section of a MACHI or CHŌ. In this case the kanji for CHŌ is only a part of that for MACHI or CHŌ given above. ME means EYE.
番地 BAN-CHI	A BAN-CHI is a section of a CHŌ-ME. BAN means NUMBER, and CHI means GROUND or PLOT.
号 GŌ	This is the smallest subdivision of all. This kanji also means NUMBER.

The actual words, CHŌME, BANCHI and GŌ are often omitted and indeed the tendency to use arabic numerals alone for the tail end of an address has been reinforced by a recent official reform. This means that what was once a clumsy 4丁目3番地 1号 is gradually becoming a handy 4の3の1. The simplified form of the example given is read YON-NO-SAN-NO-ICHI. The phonetic symbol between the numerals is NO, (sometimes the KATAKANA form ノ is used), and means OF. In Japanese it refers backwards, not forwards, so that the translation would be (literally) ONE OF THREE OF FOUR.

It is really better not to translate any of the above components of addresses.

(TŌKYŌ AND KYŌTO)

The capital of Japan used to be KYŌTO. The name, KYŌTO, is written with two kanji which both mean CAPITAL or METROPOLIS:

京　都 KYŌ-TO

When the capital was changed to what is now TŌKYŌ (formerly EDO), in the east of Japan, the kanji for EAST was added on to the front of the name of the old capital, making EAST KYŌTO, or TŌKYŌ-TO:

東京都 TŌ-KYŌ-TO

For administrative purposes, and for postal addresses written in kanji, the full name is used. But more ordinarily the modern capital is now referred to as TŌKYŌ:

東　京 TŌ-KYŌ

KYŌTO, the old capital, now has the status of a CITY (SHI):

京都市 KYŌ-TO-SHI

(TITLES)

The Japanese word SAN, for MR., MRS. or MISS, is well known. But the kanji usually appended to names on envelopes, with the same meaning, is pronounced SAMA:

様　SAMA

On occasion you may also see the two kanji

for SENSEI, which, in a rather wide sense, means TEACHER:

先　生　SEN-SEI

Two other common titles corresponding to MR. after names in writing are

殿　DONO　　and 氏 SHI

A letter addressed to husband and wife together may be graced with a more complicated formulation, like this:

MR. and MRS. 御夫妻 GO-FU-SAI

The map on the facing page shows some of the chief cities of Japan. The key to the numbers follows below.

The map and the key together may be used either for looking up the positions of important cities and the way in which their names are written, or, if you are already accustomed to them, for testing yourself. The kanji and the romanised forms of the names are in separate columns so that you may cover the latter over.

1.	小 樽	1.	OTARU
2.	札 幌	2.	SAPPORO
3.	函 館	3.	HAKODATE
4.	青 森	4.	AOMORI
5.	仙 台	5.	SENDAI
6.	新 潟	6.	NIIGATA
7.	水 戸	7.	MITO
8.	東 京	8.	TŌKYŌ
9.	横 浜	9.	YOKOHAMA
10.	鎌 倉	10.	KAMAKURA
11.	静 岡	11.	SHIZUOKA
12.	名古屋	12.	NAGOYA
13.	伊 勢	13.	ISE
14.	奈 良	14.	NARA
15.	京 都	15.	KYŌTO
16.	大 阪	16.	ŌSAKA
17.	神 戸	17.	KŌBE
18.	広 島	18.	HIROSHIMA
19.	下 関	19.	SHIMONOSEKI
20.	福 岡	20.	FUKUOKA
21.	長 崎	21.	NAGASAKI
22.	鹿児島	22.	KAGOSHIMA

二十六 GENERAL MAP XXVI

This map shows the four main islands of Japan and a few other physical landmarks. The key to the numbers follows below.

The map and key together may be used in the same way as the preceding map of chief cities.

I.	北海道	I.	HOKKAIDŌ
II.	本 州	II.	HONSHŪ
III.	四 国	III.	SHIKOKU
IV.	九 州	IV.	KYŪSHŪ

1.	大 雪 山	1.	DAISETSU-ZAN (Mt. Daisetsu)
2.	十和田湖	2.	TOWADA-KO (Lake Towada)
3.	磐 梯 山	3.	BANDAI-SAN (Mt. Bandai)
4.	浅 間 山	4.	ASAMA-YAMA (Mt. Asama)
5.	東 京 湾	5.	TŌKYŌ-WAN (Tokyo Bay)
6.	富 士 山	6.	FUJI-SAN (Mt. Fuji)
7.	伊豆半島	7.	IZU-HANTŌ (Izu Peninsula)
8.	琵 琶 湖	8.	BIWA-KO (Lake Biwa)
9.	伊 勢 湾	9.	ISE-WAN (Bay of Ise)
10.	大 阪 湾	10.	ŌSAKA-WAN (Osaka Bay)
11.	瀬戸内海	11.	SETONAIKAI (Seto Inland Sea)
12.	阿 蘇 山	12.	ASO-SAN (Mt. Aso)

日 本 海
NIHONKAI
JAPAN SEA

▲1
I

○2

▲3

▲4

II

▲6 5

7

8

9

11

10

III

IV

▲12

太 平 洋
TAIHEIYŌ
PACIFIC OCEAN

二十八   XXVII
HIRAGANA AND KATAKANA

The phonetic script used in Japan was already mentioned briefly in the INTRODUCTION. Tables giving a key to this script have been kept to the end of this booklet so that it did not seem to be a compulsory hurdle to be overcome before beginning with kanji. Moreover one end of the book or other is convenient for quick reference when you do get down to it.

Some people may find it stimulating to learn the KATAKANA first because they are used for transcribing words of foreign origin which may be familiar to the foreigner. Certain conventions have to be followed in such transcriptions which tends to make some of them a rather entertaining puzzle. For example MILK becomes ミルク (MI-RU-KU), while CAKE becomes ケーキ (KĒ-KI). Most loanwords of this kind come from English, but of course some come from other languages as well. Example: a rather nice kind of cake known as カステラ (KA-SU-TE-RA) from the Portuguese *pão de Castella*.

As for the HIRAGANA, the best way of learning them is on train journeys. Large signboards on each station give the name of the station in KANJI, in HIRAGANA and in Roman letters too. Use the romanised version to work out the HIRA-GANA; then as you progress read the HIRAGANA first and check with the Roman letters to make sure you have got them right. From a crowded train the big central signboards are sometimes invisible. But if you have been doing your practice you will be able to see where you are from vertical blue plates fixed to the pillars, which give the name of the station in HIRAGANA only. How convenient not to be completely illiterate!

Tables of HIRAGANA and KATAKANA follow, and the following points should be noted.

a) The sign ˚ hardens the consonant of the syllable concerned, making "ka" (か) into "ga" (が), etc., as shown in the tables.

b) The sign ° makes "ha" (は) into "pa" (ぱ), etc.

c) The symbols や, ゆ and よ, when written slightly smaller than the rest of the line, have a special effect on pronunciation. They really replace the vowel of the preceding syllable; and in fact that vowel is omitted in romanisation. For example, きょ is romanised as "kyo". It should be carefully distinguished from きよ, romanised as "kiyo".

d) The symbol つ, when written slightly smaller than the rest of the line, also has a special effect. In romanised form this is shown by doubling the consonant; e.g. ちょっとまって (meaning: "Wait a moment!") is transcribed as "chotto matte". In English a double consonant sounds no different from a single one, but in Japanese the pronunciation is quite different. The word is, so to speak, held up

73

for a moment. We can express it in print by hyphenating as follows (the consonants on each side of the hyphen to be pronounced separately): "chot-to mat-te". But the best way to get it right is to ask a Japanese friend to demonstrate.

e) One more symbol which sometimes has a special function is う. It is used in some cases to lengthen the vowel of the preceding syllable. For example, こ (ko) may be lengthened to こう (kō), きょ (kyo) to きょう (kyō), etc. The difference between such short and long vowels is very important in the pronunciation of Japanese. Ask a friend to pronounce the name of the city, Kyōto (京都), which, in HIRAGA-NA, would be written きょうと.

f) The above notes apply both to HIRAGANA and to KATAKANA. In the case of foreign words transcribed in KATAKANA the lengthening of a vowel is usually shown by an extended dash, as in ケーキ (kēki, meaning "cake").

HIRAGANA (CURSIVE SYLLABARY)

あ a	い i	う u	え e	お o
か ka	き ki	く ku	け ke	こ ko
さ sa	し shi	す su	せ se	そ so
た ta	ち chi	つ tsu	て te	と to
な na	に ni	ぬ nu	ね ne	の no
は ha	ひ hi	ふ fu	へ he	ほ ho
ま ma	み mi	む mu	め me	も mo
や ya	(い i)	ゆ yu	(え e)	よ yo
ら ra	り ri	る ru	れ re	ろ ro
わ wa	ゐ* i	う u	ゑ* e	を wo
ん n				

* obsolete

が ga	ぎ gi	ぐ gu	げ ge	ご go
ざ za	じ ji	ず zu	ぜ ze	ぞ zo
だ da	ぢ ji	づ zu	で de	ど do
ば ba	び bi	ぶ bu	べ be	ぼ bo
ぱ pa	ぴ pi	ぷ pu	ぺ pe	ぽ po

きゃ kya	きゅ kyu	きょ kyo
しゃ sha	しゅ shu	しょ sho
ちゃ cha	ちゅ chu	ちょ cho
にゃ nya	にゅ nyu	にょ nyo
ひゃ hya	ひゅ hyu	ひょ hyo
みゃ mya	みゅ myu	みょ myo
りゃ rya	りゅ ryu	りょ ryo

ぎゃ gya	ぎゅ gyu	ぎょ gyo
じゃ ja	じゅ ju	じょ jo
ぢゃ ja	ぢゅ ju	ぢょ jo

びゃ bya	びゅ byu	びょ byo

ぴゃ pya	ぴゅ pyu	ぴょ pyo

KATAKANA (SQUARE SYLLABARY)

ア a	カ ka	サ sa	タ ta	ナ na	ハ ha	マ ma	ヤ ya	ラ ra	ワ wa	ン n
イ i	キ ki	シ shi	チ chi	ニ ni	ヒ hi	ミ mi	(イ) i	リ ri	ヰ* i	
ウ u	ク ku	ス su	ツ tsu	ヌ nu	フ fu	ム mu	ユ yu	ル ru	ウ u	
エ e	ケ ke	セ se	テ te	ネ ne	ヘ he	メ me	(エ) e	レ re	ヱ* e	
オ o	コ ko	ソ so	ト to	ノ no	ホ ho	モ mo	ヨ yo	ロ ro	ヲ wo	

ガ ga	ザ za	ダ da	バ ba	パ pa
ギ gi	ジ ji	ヂ ji	ビ bi	ピ pi
グ gu	ズ zu	ヅ zu	ブ bu	プ pu
ゲ ge	ゼ ze	デ de	ベ be	ペ pe
ゴ go	ゾ zo	ド do	ボ bo	ポ po

* obsolete

キャ kya	キュ kyu	キョ kyo
シャ sha	シュ shu	ショ sho
チャ cha	チュ chu	チョ cho
ニャ nya	ニュ nyu	ニョ nyo
ヒャ hya	ヒュ hyu	ヒョ hyo
ミャ mya	ミュ myu	ミョ myo
リャ rya	リュ ryu	リョ ryo

ギャ gya	ギュ gyu	ギョ gyo
ジャ ja	ジュ ju	ジョ jo
ヂャ ja	ヂュ ju	ヂョ jo
ビャ bya	ビュ byu	ビョ byo
ピャ pya	ピュ pyu	ピョ pyo